The Burden of Being Me

Mayven

Publishers: Harvard Ink

Copyright © 2025 Mayven

All rights reserved.

ISBN: 978-1-0370-3594-4

First Published in 2025 by Harvard Ink—www.harvardink.com.

The content contained within this book may not be reproduced, duplicated, or transmitted without direct written permission from the author or the publisher.

Under no circumstances will any blame or legal responsibility be held against the publisher, or author, for any damages, reparation, or monetary loss due to the information contained within this book, either directly or indirectly.

Legal Notice:

This book is copyright protected. It is only for personal use. You cannot amend, distribute, sell, use, quote or paraphrase any part, or the content within this book, without the consent of the author or publisher.

Disclaimer Notice:

Please note the information contained within this document is for educational and entertainment purposes only. All effort has been executed to present accurate, up to date, reliable, complete information. No warranties of any kind are declared or implied. Readers acknowledge that the author is not engaged in the rendering of legal, financial, medical, or professional advice. Please consult a licensed professional before attempting any techniques outlined in this book.

This is a work of creative nonfiction. The events are portrayed to the best of the author's recollection and from the author's perspective. While all the stories in this book are true, names have been changed to protect the privacy of the people involved.

The conversations in the book all come from the author's memories, though they are not written to represent word-for-

word transcripts. Rather, the author has retold them in a way that evokes the feelings and meanings of what was said in all instances, rendering the essence of the dialogue accurate.

By reading this document, the reader agrees that under no circumstances is the author responsible for any losses, direct or indirect, that are incurred as a result of the use of the information contained within this document, including, but not limited to, errors, omissions, or inaccuracies.

Dedication

This book was made possible with the help of some special people whom I would sincerely like to thank:

Denzyl Janneker - Though we have not seen each other in a long time and the distance between us is great, you graciously took time from your busy schedule to help me. I am deeply thankful for your kindness and generosity.

Martin Bowler - I'm grateful for the time you spent listening, advising, and guiding me through this entire process. Your unwavering support and encouragement have been a constant source of encouragement to me.

Tyriq Bowler - Thank you for being my inspiration, my muse and my greatest cheerleader.

Daphne Kinsey - Your timely encouragement provided the final push I needed to cross the finish line when I was wavering. I am deeply grateful for your support and love.

Prologue

In the tapestry of life, some threads gleam with the promise of adventure and freedom, while others pull tight with the weight of our struggles. For me, the dream of becoming a flight attendant wasn't just about exploring the skies; it was about escaping the scars of an abusive existence and finding a way to rise above the pain of oppression and restrictions. The dream of travel became my beacon of hope—a way to break free from the chains of my past and redefine who I was.

But as with all great dreams, reality quickly revealed that the path to freedom wasn't as simple as I imagined. The skies, though vast, were filled with their own set of challenges. Each flight became a test of my resilience, each new destination a puzzle to solve. Alongside moments of laughter, there were times of terror, vulnerability, and the haunting memories of my past that I couldn't outrun.

This book is a testament to the power of survival and the strength we find when we refuse to let our pasts define us. It's a story of resilience, love, and the unyielding spirit that emerges when we face our darkest moments. If you've ever struggled with abuse, or simply found yourself caught in the weight of life's burdens, this book will remind you that the strength to rise is already within you. It's not just my story—it's a reflection of the strength we all carry, even when we can't see it.

Growing up, my life was a series of battles—a test of endurance against abuse and hardship that left marks on both my body and soul. My father's rage was unpredictable, his fists and words cutting deeper than any physical wound could. He was the kind of man who would tear through the house like a hurricane, destroying everything in his path, including our spirit. And yet, we stayed—my mother clinging to a fragile belief that things could change. Each bruise and scar told a story of survival, but the memories haunted me more than any mark on my skin ever could.

Trust was a fragile thing, shattered too many times by people who were supposed to care for me. I became an expert at hiding pain, masking it with humour and defiance, but beneath it all, I was a young girl desperately searching for someone—anyone—to tell me it wasn't my fault. Every moment of abuse, every act of betrayal, chipped away at the little innocence I had left, shaping me into someone hardened yet deeply vulnerable. This is where my story begins: in the shadows of pain and resilience, where I learned that strength isn't the absence of fear, but the courage to keep moving forward despite it.

Through my journey, I invite you to discover your own resilience, heal from the past, and find the freedom that lies within you.

Through the trials and tribulations, the laughter and the tears, I learned that the burden of being me was not something I could escape. It was a part of my journey, shaping me into the person I am today. This is my story, a testament to resilience, love, and the unyielding spirit that refuses to be broken.

Chapter 1: In the Beginning

Ever since I was young and as far back as I can remember, I have always wanted to travel. I have wanted to travel as much and as far and wide as possible. I have always harboured a deep desire to explore the world, yearning to journey to distant lands and immerse myself in diverse cultures. The thought of traversing vast landscapes, from the sun-drenched beaches of the Mediterranean to the majestic night life of Asia, and the marvellous mysteries of the Middle East fills me with an exhilarating sense of freedom and adventure. Each destination, with its unique blend of history, tradition, and natural beauty, beckons me to uncover its secrets and stories.

The allure of travel lies not just in the destinations themselves, but in the experiences and connections made along the way. Meeting new people, tasting exotic cuisines, and witnessing breathtaking sights enriches my understanding of the world and broadens my horizons. Every journey, whether to a bustling metropolis or a tranquil village, offers a chance to learn, grow, and create unforgettable memories.

In essence, my passion for travel is driven by an insatiable curiosity and a profound appreciation for the beauty and diversity of our planet. My dream was to become a flight attendant or as it was known back then, an air hostess. Most importantly, my dream was just to get away from home and from my life! The horrible, painful, sadistic life that I was living. A pain so deep from years of physical and psychological abuse that it left scars not only on my body but also on my soul. This relentless torment stunted my emotional growth, creating barriers to trust and intimacy. The wounds inflicted by this abuse are not easily healed and has cast long shadows over all my future relationships. I have a fear of vulnerability, and an inability to fully connect with others. Healing from such profound hurt requires immense strength, support, and time, as the journey to reclaim my sense of self and ability to love is fraught with challenges.

The desire to travel became the beacon of hope that fuelled my imagination and ambition. Little did I know that the burden of being me would follow me everywhere I went.

I was and always have been a fat kid who grew up to be a big girl and a voluptuous woman. Being a curvy goddess means I never have to worry about disappearing in a crowd. Sure, finding clothes that fit can sometimes feel like navigating through a fashion minefield, but it just adds a little excitement to my shopping expeditions. And then there is online shopping, oh the joyful hours I have spent browsing the thousands of pages of beautiful and stylish clothes and shoes at my leisure and pure pleasure! And let's not forget the undeniable perks: extra cushioning for cozy cuddles, and everyone knows big girls bring their A-game to the dance floor!

So much for being a flight attendant though, since the criteria were very strict and specific when it came to body type and size. I was forever on some kind of diet or other and one exercise regime after another. However, willpower was sorely lacking in my genetic makeup. To me, food was more enticing, exciting, and comforting than a sexy body. And food is my mom's love language. If you are feeling sick, happy, sad, down, or even bored, she would feed you! But even to this day, I am still trying to follow every new exercise trend, without compromising on my food though. I like food. I like cooking it and I like eating it. Food has always been more than just sustenance; it is an enticing adventure that excites all my senses and brings immense comfort to my soul. The vibrant colours, tantalizing aromas, and exquisite flavours evoke a sense of exhilaration that surpasses the superficial allure of a mere good-looking body. My friend Marvin is a brilliant, self-taught chef who is always eager to showcase his culinary skills, and I'm more than happy to serve as the taste tester for his new recipes. Likewise, my husband Kent takes great pride in his cooking mastery, so who am I to refuse or complain when they are eager to feed me? And the saying goes: "Fat people are happy people". Well, at least while we're eating!

In addition to the strict body type and size requirements for becoming a flight attendant, I did not meet the criteria due to the colour of my skin. I grew up during the apartheid era in South Africa, where Coloured individuals were barred from many job opportunities designated for "Whites Only".

Flight attendant was one of those jobs. The apartheid system created social and economic challenges for the Coloured communities and led to the formation of racially segregated townships where the people were isolated from economic opportunities. This marginalisation gave rise to helplessness and left a community of many men who drank their sorrows away daily. With alcohol often came aggression. The violent tendencies that developed in many households were a tragic consequence of the systemic abuse and alienation we faced. In a society where men were stripped of their roles as providers and protectors, their frustration often turned inward—and, more often than not, outward. Physical abuse, especially domestic violence, was common. Ultimately this led to a community with many abusive homes and many families who were too embarrassed to speak about their shameful secrets. Had we just known that we were all suffering the same injustices, we could have all come together and helped each other. But back then, these things were never discussed openly!

Another escape I had from my dreary life was reading. I would often go to the local library and borrow three or four books at a time and then read until the early hours of the morning, under the blankets, with a torch. Sometimes, I would get caught and get scolded or punished, and my books would be confiscated for a few days.

So the threads that kept me human during the times of extreme stress were my dreams of travel, food, and books.

Chapter 2: Lasting Bonds

I grew up in a township called Wentworth in KwaZulu-Natal, south of Durban, in South Africa. We lived in a double-storey, semi-detached house in a street where everybody knew everybody. There was a huge church at the top of the street and a playground with swings and a seesaw midway next to a power station. The community was so big that the primary school had to be split into two sessions with some kids going to morning school and the rest going to afternoon school. I was in the afternoon school.

High school for me was great. Maths and Accounting were by far my worst subjects, so I dropped those very early on and the rest were quite manageable, so I didn't struggle academically. I even received awards of excellence for my language subjects. I loved Geography. I was a physically strong girl who took part in sports like shot put and javelin and ran the 800-meter race in school. I wasn't built for speed, but I did have endurance. I was in the choir and chess club. I was by no means a nerd though. I just wasn't clever enough for that! Being a bigger girl, I was naughty and did stupid things to fit in with the popular girls sometimes, but eventually, that was not important to me. I liked to think of myself as kind-hearted and didn't like mistreating and teasing other kids like they did. Or being rude to some of the teachers for no reason. I always rooted for the underdog.

I was quite popular with the boys though. I used to hang out with a group of guys who rode motorbikes to school and would pick me up and take me home after school. They even taught me how to ride. I was so afraid of getting caught because if my mom knew, she would have skinned me alive! Once, I was getting off the motorbike outside the school in the morning and I leaned too close to the scorching hot exhaust pipe. It left the skin of my calf behind. It hurt like a thousand needles were piercing my skin at the same time. When I got home that night I had to lie to my mom and say that it was an accident in the Home Economics class that day and she felt so sorry for me she tried to nurse me back to health. Until she found out the real story. Then trouble rained down on me.

And boy was I clumsy, oh my word! The number of times I embarrassed myself in public in the silliest of ways is almost too many to count. From tripping over my own feet in the middle of a crowded street to accidentally waving back at someone who wasn't actually waving at me, my life seems to be a series of comical mishaps. Each of these moments, while mortifying at the time, has become a cherished memory that I can laugh about now. They remind me not to take myself too seriously and to embrace the humour in life's little blunders. After all, it's these silly, embarrassing moments that make life interesting and give us stories to tell our kids and grandkids. And my clumsiness was by no means limited to the school grounds only!

My English teacher, Mr Williamson, always encouraged me to write a book because he thought he saw potential in me from a young age. "You need to nurture this talent from as early as possible," he said. "I will always be here to help you," he promised. I did start with a book, and my mom even bought me a typewriter. But my home life was just too volatile at the time to concentrate on a long-term project like that.

I met him again at our 20-year school reunion and the first thing he asked me was: "How many books have you written so far?" Unfortunately, my response had to be "Sadly Sir, none." You could see the disappointment in his face.

My Afrikaans teacher also thought rather highly of me but that was because I was probably the best student in her subject in the entire grade. Durban is primarily an English-speaking community, but my gran and dad come from an Afrikaans-speaking family and have always only spoken Afrikaans to me. I guess this helped me a lot in school.

At the age of twelve, my mom took my brother and I and went to live in Nigel, Gauteng with my aunt Rose, one of my mom's older sisters. This was a result of the abuse from my dad.

Bear in mind that I am a Durban girl where winter warrants a thin, knitted cardigan to keep one comfortable. Durban is a major city located on the east coast of South Africa with a moderate climate all year round. Moving just East of Johannesburg (one of the highest major cities in the world at approximately 1 753 meters above sea level) was a bit of a shock to a warm-weather girl. Winter in Nigel requires that you wear seventeen layers of jerseys, jackets, hoodies, coats, scarves, and beanies, just to survive the icy cold weather! At night you had to sleep under four or five blankets and duvets, while wearing flannel pyjamas underneath a polyester tracksuit. And although the school was not far from our house, it was the longest walk ever during the six months of winter. The classrooms were heated with coal stoves, and I always tried to sit closest to that heat source.

Aunt Rose and her husband Ivan moved to Nigel for his job. His brother and his family also moved there for the same reason. Later, Ivan's sister followed with her kids due to marital issues. And that is how we all ended up in this little town. From the three households we were nine kids in total to begin with, and we all became very good friends. Our parents were friends with each other even before they all got married. Eventually my mother and brother returned to Durban, while I stayed in Nigel for the remaining nine months of the school year.

My friends Brody and Dora also lived there, as well as their cousins, one of whom tragically died in a drowning incident during our stay. They were the kids of my uncle's siblings. Without my mom around, I felt like an orphan. Everyone else had parents, but even though my aunt treated me like her own child since she didn't have any, she wasn't a replacement for my mom. Although all three households were close and lived nearby to each other and did almost everything together, I still longed and worried for my family.

In all honesty, I did not miss the violence and the constant barrage of expletives being screamed at us. It was always quite peaceful and harmonious. There were never any fights or arguments at Aunt Rose's place, but I could not help but wonder what my mom was going through on her own, without me there to protect her.

During the summer months, we kids used to walk to the movies on Saturdays and pay fifty cents for a double feature, it was only Chinese Karate movies but we loved them. Occasionally on Wednesday nights my aunt would take us to the drive-in theatre in Springs, to watch the latest blockbuster movies. This was the closest town to where we lived. It was a very small town and community with very little to do, so we had to find our own entertainment and fun.

My playmates found their entertainment in me. I must admit, when it comes to fears, spiders take the cake for me. I mean, these eight-legged creatures seem like they were designed by some evil genius just to terrorise innocent souls like mine. And let me tell you, Brody, Dora, and their cousins didn't help alleviate my arachnid anxiety one bit. I became their entertainment. Our house was opposite an open field, and they would go in there and catch spiders and chase me. They gleefully watched me unravel into a state of unbridled hysteria as I would run around shrieking like a lunatic, "No, no, no, stay away from me," through the neighbourhood. And they would be squealing in delight with laughter.

It was in this same field that we decided to start a fire one day and I happened to be standing downwind when a burning piece of plastic was airlifted and blown onto my ankle. It just stuck there and melted into my skin. Instantly, I felt intense pain and frantically tried to rip off the scorching item. But it wouldn't come off without taking my skin with it. It had melted into my flesh. The pain was excruciating but I refused to cry. I could not give the other kids a reason to tease me. I had a reputation to uphold, an image to maintain. I was the eldest kid there after all. When my aunt saw how bad the burn was, she freaked out! Without wasting a second, she rushed me to the doctor. She was genuinely shocked by the severity of the injury. Moral of the story: don't play with fire, you will definitely get burnt! It was one of many visits to the doctor for me during that year.

Our fun extended to some rather unexpected pursuits. At one point the municipality was installing new underground water systems in the area. So, these huge concrete drainage pipes were lined up alongside the road where the trenches were being dug. Somehow, we thought it would be fun to push one of these pipes, which were two meters long with a diameter of about sixty centimetres, up a hill, climb into it rolled up like a letter C, and then roll down the hill. We were packed tighter than a can of sardines and I was at one end. As we descended the hill, I decided that I had had enough, and I needed to get out immediately! The feeling of claustrophobia closed in on me from all sides and the dizziness from the constant rotations, like being in a tumble dryer, was nauseating. This carnival ride turned from fun to frightening very fast. The tears were streaming down my face or rather, tears were flying out of my eyes! I put my hand out and held onto the edge of the rolling pipe which inevitably rolled over my fingers. For some reason I did not think to let go of the pipe, I just left my hand there and the pipe just repeatedly rolled over and over and over my fingers, bouncing and crushing them with each turn until eventually we reached the bottom of the hill, and we came to a sudden jarring halt. Everyone else was screaming in glee and elation while I was screaming in anguish and agony looking at my flat fingers and thumb. There were little stones and debris stuck in them, mixed with blood and dirt. My stomach was tied in knots and my legs felt like cooked spaghetti. And so, we were off to the doctor again!

Aunt Rose and I had such a good relationship with the doctor and the pharmacist by now that we were on a first-name basis. Sometimes I got hurt in such stupid ways doing such silly things that I wouldn't even bother to tell her because I was so embarrassed. I was just being an unnecessary expense, so I would secretly nurse myself back to health. Until the next time. I had cuts and bruises and scars all over my body, like a naughty boy who couldn't resist the call of adventure. Each mark told a story of my fearless escapades and mischievous exploits. Each of these marks was a badge of honour, a testament to my boundless energy and unquenchable thirst for adventure. They were the physical evidence of a childhood spent exploring, pushing boundaries, and living life to the fullest.

There was a boy who lived next door who just thought that I was the bee's knees and would do anything for me. Desmond! He used to write me love letters and dress up in a suit to bring me flowers. He followed me around incessantly and would bring me fruit and sweets all the time. My uncle's work contract expired, so I left Nigel and went back to Durban at the end of that year. Desmond continued to write letters to me. He, Brody, and Dora were my salvation during that time.

But if there was one person who truly doted on me, it was my cousin Kenny. He was the son of my mom's eldest sister. He spent a lot of time at my house and in fact at all his relatives' houses. He was very filial. He was the most fearless and feared gangster of his time, yet to me he was the gentlest and kindest soul who cared for me and worried about me and saw and felt my pain and loneliness. A gangster who would take the time to sit and comb my hair gently while talking to me about nothing and everything or read books to me when he had the chance. He wrote letters to my mom telling her of my well-being and of my sorrow. These I would find only when I returned home a year later.

He worked in Sasolburg on shutdowns and would make the effort to come to Nigel to visit me on his weekends off. He only worked during shutdowns. This is when companies would halt operations of an industrial plant or oil refinery to do maintenance for a certain period.

I was twelve and he was in his late twenties or early thirties. He cared for me and protected me like a younger sister. His love and his warmth shielded me from the harsh realities of my life. At least when he was around. I lived for the days when he would come around. Actually, I would just look forward to anyone coming to visit quite frankly, because it provided some respite from my dreary existence, especially back in Durban.

It was the year I completed standard 9, or grade 11. I remember that during the week my report was due to arrive by post, Kenny was busy painting our house for my mom, and my father didn't go to work that week. I watched for the postman like a hawk, terrified that my father might get the report before I did. If I had failed, I knew I would face severe consequences, so I had to make sure I got it first. I watched vigilantly all week long. But on Friday afternoon, I stepped away for a few minutes to visit my aunt, who lived down the road just a few houses away. Just then, Kenny came looking for me, dressed in his paint-stained overalls. Worriedly he said: "The Postman was just here, and your old man took your report from him." He looked at me intently and I looked back with wide eyes, holding my breath, waiting for the next words out of his mouth. Finally, he said: "He sent him to fetch you 'coz you failed. He's gonna whip you."

I was devastated! I thought that I had put a lot of effort into my studies and did not deserve to be beaten because I could not make it. I wanted to cry, and I wanted to stay at my aunt's place until my mom got home but Kenny insisted that I had to go home immediately.

As we were walking back up the road and I was biting my lower lip and ringing my hands, he started laughing and pulled out the sealed, brown envelope from inside his overalls, and handed it to me. "I was just teasing you; I managed to get the envelope from the postman before he even reached the house," he said. I hurriedly opened the envelope and saw that I actually did pass the final exam and would be starting matric the following year. The happiness and relief were overwhelming, and Kenny shared my joy and celebration with me. We jumped and danced and screamed in the middle of the street like two maniacs. I loved him dearly!

A few weeks later, on Christmas Eve, he was murdered, and my ray of warm sunshine was gone.

Our life was like that. Just a part of the harsh context of being Coloured in South Africa back then. There had been many instances Kenny's life where he had been really badly injured in an attack or fight and everyone thought he would never make it due to the severity of his wounds. Sometimes he would have multiple wounds, but he would always pull through. On this specific occasion, he stepped out of his house and received one single stab wound to his heart and just died. He was so handsome, short, and agile, and had been through so much. Yes, he did do things that gangsters do, but to me he was loving, kind, gentle, devoted, caring, tender, and considerate.

And for many months thereafter the half-painted house remained exactly as he had left it before he died.

Chapter 3: Lifelines

I had some of the best friends and people in my life, maybe because of my circumstances I was blessed in this way. Whatever the reason, I am so grateful and am happy to still have some of them in my life even now. There were our next-door neighbours, their son's name was Ethan, who helped us out of a lot of sticky situations and provided refuge for me on many occasions.

Ethan and I were neighbours since we were little kids. Their family never had a vehicle, so we were always there to transport them wherever they needed to go. From a very young age, his mom always taught him to greet me like a little sister, by kissing me on my forehead. And that is how we have always grown up, like little sister and older brother.

And of course, there was Brody, for whom I will be eternally indebted because what might seem to be a small and insignificant thing to him or to someone else, was such a profound act of strength and kindness at a time when I needed it the most. He and his sister Dora are a huge part of my life, and I cannot imagine it without them! And my best friend Morgan who was always there to listen to my sob stories and sit and discuss ridiculous and impossible revenge plots for hours and hours for many years. We would even steal my father Norman's alcohol in later years when we started drinking ourselves. Morgan was younger than me, but she was so beautiful, strong, and confident. I was inexplicably drawn to her the moment I laid eyes on her, for she exuded a magnetic aura of unwavering confidence that seemed to radiate from every pore. It was as if she possessed an intangible charm that effortlessly commanded attention and admiration.

In contrast, my own self-doubt had always held me back, chaining me in the clutches of insecurity. Yet, in her presence, I found myself irresistibly drawn like a moth to a flame —eager to learn the secrets behind her unrivalled self-assuredness. Morgan's parents welcomed me into their home with open arms. We went to the same high school and if I was on time in the morning, I would get a free ride to school with them. Morgan was not just any ordinary person, but rather a powerful force that kept me grounded and preserved my sanity. Her presence in my life was like a lifeline, always ensuring that I remained intact, mentally and emotionally. She possessed a rare ability to understand me on a level that few others could comprehend, always knowing when I needed her unwavering support or even just a comforting presence.

There was a mischievous boy named Terry who lived around the corner from my house, and he was about the same age as me. He was relentless in his dogged pursuit of me. Every time I stepped through the gate, he would be waiting to steal a kiss from me. I was such a tomboy, and shy, so I would never allow it. I would sprint back home whenever I saw him. But he was determined, and he would chase me all the way right back home. I would burst through the front door, my parents sitting in the lounge, with him hot on my heels. He would tell them with conviction, "I will marry your daughter soon." This had become a game for him and an irritation for me.

My mom thought this was cute and innocent. He was just one of those neighbourhood naughty boys, you know? Not the type to be disrespectful or mean, but definitely mischievous and always up to some kind of trickery. He had a knack for pushing boundaries and finding new ways to stir up trouble, all in good fun. Whether it was pulling pranks on unsuspecting neighbours or brazenly teasing older folks, he thrived on the thrill of breaking minor rules. But what set him apart was his undeniable charm and infectious laughter, that made everyone forgive his naughty antics. It wasn't long before everyone grew fond of his playful nature, channelling their own inner child when he was around. Sometimes it's refreshing to have someone like him around who reminds us that life can still be full of mischief and laughter, without being rude or nasty. Plus, he was cute!

I, with my magnificently substantial physique, managed to attract a group of young gentlemen in the neighbourhood. Oh yes, it appeared that my ample curves and generous proportions were simply too magnetic for these lads to resist. I think the issue was that in out neighbourhood that was a serious lack of girls and way too many boys. This meant that there were always multiple boys interested in the same girl at the same time. But the "Miss Tomboy" just wanted to play soccer, kennicky, harbour in the air, hide-and-seek, and skateboard with them. They used to pay my younger brother fifty cents for an opportunity to talk to me and he would make lots of empty promises whilst filling his pockets. And I would never show up for these little rendezvous because I knew nothing about them to begin with. Sometimes Ervin would trick me into being at certain places at certain times and make it look like a coincidence that I ran into whomever he made the deal with.

Back then we played made-up games out in the streets all day long, until the streetlights came on. We lived on a street that was perhaps a 25-degree incline and I loved competing with the boys when they were skateboarding down that road. My knees and chest were always aching from the tar burns I got when I fell off of the skateboard. My mom never bought me pants or shorts, only lacy dresses and frilly skirts, as if by dressing me girly she could make me more like her idea of a daughter. But the road rash didn't stop me—I kept launching myself down the middle of the tar road despite it all, no matter how many times I had to pick gravel out of my skin afterward. In one instance when I was fifteen, I was wearing a pink, strap dress; standing on the skateboard going downhill at high speed from the top of the street. One of the boys was standing at the bottom end where the road curved to the left out of view, so that he could warn us if there were any cars approaching and as luck would have it, there was. Now in a situation like that, your choices were to head straight for the car or jump off the high-speed skateboard. The choice was obvious, I jumped off the high-speed skateboard and the inertia kept me running down that road while the gravity pulled me down onto the tar onto my stomach and I skidded for a good two-to-three meters. At least I had the good sense to keep my head elevated, but when I stood up, the straps from my dress had snapped, and the dress had rolled down to my waist. I was standing there topless, and the dress had rolled down into a skirt. The skin on my chest and stomach were raw, what we called back then polony because it was pink like the sandwich meat. I was flat-chested, so it didn't bother me because I was one of the boys and everyone was gawking at my polony, my battle scars, not at my bare chest.

Kennicky was a game that needed two bricks, a short stick sharpened on either end, and a longer stick with which to hit the shorter stick. The two bricks would be set next to each other, and the shorter stick would be sharpened at both ends so that it could bounce off the ground when hit and would sit on the bricks. You would use the longer stick to lift and fling the shorter stick as far away from the bricks as possible and then go and hit the shorter one into the air and hit it back towards the bricks. The fewer shots it would take, the better. A kind of golf game. But with sticks and bricks. The one with the least shots is the winner. We played these silly but fun games for hours. And it was very entertaining, and those kids that I played with were my escape, my happy place.

Chapter 4: Family Ties

From the outside, we were just a normal average family of four consisting of my Dad Norman, my Mom Palm, me May, and my younger brother Ervin. There was a sister between us, Leigh, but she passed away before Ervin was born. I don't remember her apart from my mom's stories and pictures.

Ervin was also born sickly and needed my mom's undivided attention from birth. This left little to no time for me since she spent most of the first year of his life in the hospital with him. And even when they came home eventually, he had to be watched like a hawk in case he relapsed or had an episode or whatever. I guess this is what has made me into the independent person that I am today. I have always had to rely on myself since there was nobody else. I was only six at the time and didn't understand that he was born with a hole in his heart, or what that even meant. But my turn would come much later in life when I developed my own heart disease. Apparently, it is hereditary. Thanks folks!

Mom is the second youngest of sixteen siblings. They grew up on a farm where Gran literally gave birth to all her kids on her own and then got up to work the land on the farm the very next day. She was a strong matriarch who managed her household well. They were well off with each child having their own personal helper. According to our ancestry, my great-great- great-grandmother was an African princess who married a Scottish man. My mother is a meek, mild, spiritual person who is protective of her kids.

A lot of abuse was inflicted upon her because of the belief she held in her faith and her commitment to her religion. "The wife must be submissive, and the husband is the head of the household" was her mantra. The mere thought of divorce did not even dare to cross her mind, not even when she discovered his unforgivable act of infidelity. It was as if the concept of separation did not exist in her world, for she had always believed in the sanctity of marriage.

Yet, amidst this betrayal, her heart bled with unbridled agony, torn between forgiveness and self-preservation. She was also not a confident person and used the excuse that she was staying for the sake of the kids. Personally, I think it was more fear than anything else. She believed that she was financially dependent on him.

She wasn't! We were not poor. And perhaps it was why I started my first business at the age of thirteen. I kept telling her that the kids don't need him, but I was "the kid" so my opinion did not count. I had witnessed firsthand the destructive impact this man had on our family, and the memories of those turbulent times are etched deeply in my mind. His presence was like a dark cloud that overshadowed our home, bringing with it a storm of chaos and pain. I remember the constant tension that filled the air, the arguments that erupted over the smallest things, and the way his actions slowly eroded the trust and love that once bound us together. Yet my pleas for understanding fell on deaf ears as my mother remained blind to the toxicity he brought into our lives. It frustrated me to no end that my perspective as the one directly affected by his actions was disregarded, as if I lacked the wisdom or insight to comprehend what was best for us just because of my age. My frustration grew with every passing day, fuelling a burning determination within me to protect my family from his detrimental violence and abuse, despite being dismissed as merely "a kid."

In contrast, my mom's sisters are all strong capable women who stand up to their husbands and who stood up for her time and time again. They supported her throughout the years of difficulties and have even beat him up on more than one occasion. Yes, I know this sounds strange but this sort of thing was quite the norm in our community.

Somehow, she always went back to him.

Looking back, the decision to stay did more harm than good as we grew into adulthood. Vowing never again to be meek, mild, abused, or battered, I have become a rather distant and self-protective person who sometimes comes across as cold and guarded. Conversely, Ervin swore to avoid becoming like our father, and in doing so, became a tender-hearted, sweet-natured man whose wife now dominates him. Ervin is a soft-hearted, kind, and generous person. He is easily taken advantage of. With his trusting heart and naive nature, he becomes the perfect target for those who see his vulnerability as an open invitation to exploit him. Because my sister died at the age of two and Ervin was born sickly, my mom doted on him for fear of losing him as well. He was brought up as a spoilt brat and I was just an extra in the TV show called Ervin. I didn't exist unless something needed cleaning, fixing, fetching, etc.

Being the older sister of a feeble but wayward and mischievous boy who was allowed to get away with murder because of his condition, I was very protective of him. Ervin and I would fight each other like cat and dog, to the point of drawing blood. It was mostly mine because I would always go easy on him.

But let someone else try to interfere with him, anyone, even our mom and I would literally see red. It was not acceptable. As my younger brother, he was mine to smack around and nobody else's.

If I love you, I will fight with you. But I will also fight for you to the death!

Ervin had an altercation with a neighbour once, I can't even remember what it was about. A grown man named Bruce! I went out and confronted him, his wife, and his mother. Needless to say, a barrage of insults and threats were exchanged, but I can be very formidable and scary when it comes to my mostest and closest, my nearest and dearest. This grown man cried like a baby! He couldn't believe that a fourteen-year-old girl could be so brazen and so harsh. Ervin was only eight at the time.

They still had the nerve to come and complain to my mom when she got home from work. She was so amused but still chastised me with a smile on her face. She liked that I protected her little boy, not so much that I smacked him when he got out of hand though.

Once she got so tired of our quarrelling and bickering that she had had enough. She told us to each go out and pick a stick from the tree and beat each other in front of her until we had had our fill. Ervin got the bigger stick because I was not taking this seriously. We stood in front of Mom in the dining room, and he started hitting me on my legs. I thought "I cannot hit this kid; I will kill him". He was enjoying himself until his blows started to sting, and I started to hit back. It took just three strikes, and he screamed like he was being skinned alive and Mom said, "Stop, stop, stop, that's enough!" I felt cheated.

All is fair in love and war, I guess. I'm not sure what the purpose of this little exercise was, but whatever it was, it did not work. There was no lesson learned. And the bickering and sibling rivalry continued for many years to come until finally my mom shipped me off to live with my Aunt Beryl in Johannesburg at the age of twenty-one, because it became unbearable for her.

As I said, from the outside, we seemed normal to people who didn't really know us. But to our neighbours and immediate family, they knew what a royal shit show we actually were. Norman was the favourite son of eight kids and an abusive alcoholic who was on a power trip. Only at home though. He would never do and say things while sober that he did while drunk or when he was in the company of other people who could possibly take him to task for his behaviour. He was quite an intelligent and manipulative man who had the most beautiful handwriting. When he was not inebriated, we could spend hours discussing the books that we had read. His favourite author was Wilbur Smith, and he loved Andy Capp and Tintin comics. We spent a lot of time quizzing each other on general knowledge and doing crossword puzzles together.

He turned everything into a competition and even went as far as arm wrestling and weightlifting with me because he could not believe how strong I was for a girl. He had an insatiable desire to prove himself superior in every aspect of life.

On the other hand, the minute he had a drink, the monster came out in him. He could not stand the sight of me. He would constantly tell me that I was not his child. Mind you, I look exactly like him, the female version of him. Big ears and all. I hated my ears throughout my childhood and well into my early twenties. They are exactly like his!

Nobody is all good or bad, and Norman was a mix of light and dark. Neither fully good nor fully bad, this can be confusing for a child. He was a plasterer by trade, with meticulously honed skills and unrivalled attention to detail, and he elevated his craft to an art form. Each stroke of his trowel was executed with precision and finesse, creating flawlessly smooth surfaces that were the envy of his peers. One of the best when he was not drinking. He did excellent work in and around our house, but he would make me do it with him, he did not like working alone. I would mix cement with a spade and hand him bricks while he was up on a scaffold. I held the wood while he attached beams to the ceiling, drilled, sawed, hammered nails, and did all sorts of handyman chores that a young boy should be doing at that age. Is it any wonder that I was not the girly type? He often said, "You should have been born a boy. I even chose the name Marcel for you before you were born. Pity you are a girl." My mom was roped in as well. He made her hoist a car engine once while he was doing an overhaul in his Chevrolet El Camino. Crazy bastard!

He would insist that I play card games or board games with him just so that he could torture my soul. I am as stubborn and hardheaded as he is and will never back down, especially if I know I am right. Or just to make sure that he doesn't get his way! It would always end in a fight with me getting a beating. I knew this, but I just could not stop myself and I just could not give in to him. Whether it was pride or stupidity, I am not sure and I don't know why I did it. But that was just his ploy to get into a fight with my mom. For the most part, she just ignored him, until he would just take it too far. Then she would react and that is exactly what he wanted and got most of the time. Mostly it would just be a huge argument but inevitably she would get a thrashing which was always his aim, his end game!

This kind of behaviour stems from him being spoiled by his mom, I think. She was a small little woman who also ruled her family with an iron fist, but she doted on my father most amongst all her kids. She was the only one who could control him. I was her favourite grandchild because I was the child of her favourite child.

When he was drunk, which was very often, he would generally go to his bedroom upstairs. Until he would hear the three of us watching TV downstairs. This was his greatest bone of contention. He would stagger down the stairs, rip out the TV cables, go back upstairs, and put them under his pillow. This was around five or six p.m.

My mum would say "Never mind, we can play cards until bedtime."

And the demon would stagger down the stairs and switch off all the lights.

My mom would wait for him to go back up and then switch them back on again.

This took a lot of effort on his part. But by the third or fourth time, he would come down with a knobkerrie (which is a stick that is carved with a wooden ball at the end of it, also known as a wooden club). Then he would just smash the light bulbs. So, we would sit in the dark and talk and tell jokes because my mom was still trying to keep our spirits up. By now he was raging mad and came down with three sjamboks (a long stiff whip normally made out of rhinoceros tail, but he also made them out of plaited fishing gut attached to a short stick). One for each of us! He would beat us senseless. This was neither the first nor the last time. At some point he decided that the whole ritual of coming down and pulling the cable out, then switching the lights off then hitting the globes out was too time consuming. Then he just started with hitting the globes out from the get-go. It was just one of the many atrocities of his twenty-year reign of terror!

And this pretty much set the tone for the rest of my life.

Chapter 5: Away from Home

The best place we visited often, mostly without Norman, was on the South Coast, Sezela.

My mom's second-eldest sister and her family lived in Sezela and it was pure bliss. Norman couldn't easily get his way when he was amongst my aunties.

Sezela is a small town on the mouth of the iSezela River in KwaZulu-Natal, South Africa. Most people who lived there worked at the sugar mill, including my aunts' husband. The house in Sezela was just across the railway lines from the beach and it was such a safe and happy place that we as kids had free reign.

We would go to the beach every day without supervision and just have a blast. Swim in the nude and harvest mussels from the rocks until the mill's security would come and chase us away. My aunt had six kids, the youngest two were closest to my age and we were best friends. We would often go on weekends when everybody from my mother's side of the family would gather, but mostly I would be sent there during the school holidays. The best time of my life!

As far as I can remember, the weather there was always sunny and warm. I do not ever recall a rainy or cold day. We spent wonderful sunny days on the beach from morning till night and only went home when we got hungry. On some days, when we did not go down to the beach, we would climb up onto the roof of the house and lie there overlooking the blue water into the horizon, and just talk about the silly things that kids talk about. The thing about Sezela is that all the adults always just sat and played cards for money, for hours and hours, and all the kids were just left to their own devices. This was where we had freedom while under "some" supervision.

Ifafa Beach was the next town over from Sezela; and my uncle and his family owned a huge property there which was shared by him and his siblings. After he had died my aunt had to move out of the sugar-mill house and back to their house in Ifafa. Ifafa is a Zulu expression meaning "Place of Sparkling Waters". The house still exists today, and my cousin still lives there. Sadly, I don't get to visit as often but that place holds the dearest memories for me. It is still the family-gathering spot for special occasions.

My gran, Norman's mom, lived on a farm called Hlutankungu for most of my childhood. It is a rural area known for its scenic landscapes and cultural heritage. It holds a rich cultural tapestry and traditions that are integral to its identity. Those were fun times because we would go there at least once a month and so would all of Norman's brothers with all my cousins from Norman's side of the family.

It was so good being around other kids my age and not having to worry about what Norman might do next. It was rare that he acted up in front of his mom. She was probably the only person that he really feared. That is so funny because she was tiny in stature, she seemed to be just a piece of a person. But she knew how to control him.

I was her favourite grandchild probably because of all the hardship I had to endure. So, I was spoiled and made to feel quite special most of the time. She would always give me extra food and snacks or sweets, take me shopping, and buy me stuff that none of the other kids would get. And she would make me promise not to tell them. And she had many grandkids!

Hlutankungu was a livestock farm and a plantation, and we would go there so that the brothers could slaughter whatever livestock they needed to take back home to the city for the month, to fill their freezers. We always had fresh meat to eat and back then we were living large because if you could eat meat every day, you were doing well! After the activities of one such weekend, we were on our way home and Norman had been drinking with his brothers before we left the farm. At the time, he was driving a 1400 Nissan bakkie with a canopy on the back. Ervin and I were at the back while Norman and my mother were in front in the cab. Norman and my mother's voices were muffled by the engine noise, but even from the back, I could feel the tension between them, thick like a storm cloud hanging overhead.

Then, without warning, Norman slammed on the brakes, the tires screeching as the van jerked to a halt on the side of the road. "Get out," he growled to my mother, his voice sharp like a blade. I barely had time to register what was happening before he was already yanking her out of the cab, pulling her roughly by the arm.

"Norman, stop!" I heard my mother protest, her voice trembling with something I couldn't quite place—fear, maybe, or disbelief. But Norman didn't listen. With a cruel laugh, he started stripping her, tearing off her clothes until she was standing there, shivering in nothing but her underwear, as though she were nothing but a thing to be discarded. The words that followed were venomous, a barrage of verbal abuse that made my stomach churn.

He liked speaking Afrikaans to her when he was angry, "Jy dink jy's slim" *(You think you're clever)* Norman spat, his face twisted in anger, his eyes wild. His words hit her like punches, but there was no stopping him. With a grunt, he shoved her towards the edge of a steep cliff, a drop that seemed endless, the shadows of the evening stretching long and cold at the bottom. And then—*he threw her*.

My breath caught in my chest as I watched her stumble, her body crumpling as she fell, disappearing into the dark void below. My heart pounded, and my feet felt like they were glued to the back of the bakkie. I couldn't move. Couldn't breathe.

Then a sharp voice cut through the horror. "Mom!" I screamed, my feet moving before my brain could process it. I scrambled out of the back of the bakkie and ran—ran as fast as I could, desperate to stop this nightmare. The dual carriageway ahead was empty, but I threw myself into the middle of it, arms flailing, hoping someone would see me, hoping someone would stop.

There was not a single car on the road but still I cried and begged. "Please!" I screamed at the top of my lungs, "Help! Somebody, please!"

The first car full of young Indian men swerved past me and just carried on while I was crying and screaming at them to stop. I was about ten or eleven at the time and this was around 1978 when apartheid was still at its peak. So, any kind of involvement between the races wasn't the norm. Indians did not talk to, or help, Coloureds.

The next car that came along had an elderly White couple in it. They were old! When they stopped, I didn't think that they would be able to help at all. But I guess Norman still had respect for the White man because he suddenly became a very timid person while this little old lady told my mom to climb up the cliff. I took her clothes and formed a rope to help her out while the man kept Norman away by just standing in front of him, and when my mom got to the top the old lady helped her get dressed. They put the three of us in their car and drove us to the nearest police station. I will forever be grateful to that couple because if they did not come by at that moment, God only knows what the outcome would have been. However, going to the police station was just a temporary measure because Norman followed us, and he wasn't even arrested. The police just let us leave with him and he proceeded to beat my mother all the way home. That ride took about thirty minutes, a very long thirty minutes.

On many occasions I would beg my mom to leave but she just wouldn't do it. And to this day I will never understand why. No, not why, I will never understand the unnatural fear she had of him.

As I mentioned before, one time she did manage to leave when I was twelve. That's when we went to her sister in Nigel, Gauteng. We stayed there for three months before he came to fetch her and my brother. He forced her to go home with him by torturing her. He put out lit cigarettes on her arms while they were in bed at night and threatened her, telling her to not to make a sound so that she did not alert my aunt and uncle. Ervin and I were sleeping on the floor in the same bedroom and heard everything. He made all kinds of threats until eventually she conceded and left with him. On the day they were leaving, I begged her not to go.

"Mom please" I begged "He tortured you all of last night, what makes you think it will be better when you get back home?"

"He promised" she said. "I think he means it this time."

"You know he doesn't. He never means it; he is going to do the same thing again and again. Mom please don't go," I cried.

She was leaving under duress and if he was taking her

home under the pretence of being a changed man while having tortured her the night before. You can only imagine what lie in store for her back home. I even stood in front of the car in the middle of the street arms and legs spread wide as if I could stop them. Aunt Rose had to come and drag me away out of the street. I was heartbroken, wondering if I would ever see them again! And this is how at the age of twelve I ended up in Nigel with my Aunt Rose and Uncle Ivan for one year.

When I was sixteen, we took a trip to Johannesburg to visit my mom's sister, Beryl. The journey from Durban to Johannesburg was a long one—about six hours on the road—but we didn't mind. Aunt Rose and her husband came along too, driving in their own car, so the road trip was filled with conversation, jokes, and the familiar hum of the tires on the asphalt. I remember the excitement of seeing my aunts and cousins and the warmth of being around family, even if there was always that quiet unease when Norman was around.

We spent the day out, visiting various places around Johannesburg, but by late afternoon, it was time to head back. On our way home, we decided to stop at a supermarket to grab a few groceries for dinner. My mom was in Beryl's car, staying behind because Beryl's baby had fallen asleep. We were all in the other cars, piling out and heading into the store. When we returned, the first thing that struck me was the crowd. A huge group of people had gathered around the three cars in the parking lot, and a tense silence had settled over the scene. My heart sank as I saw Norman standing near the car where my mom was. He had pulled her out of Beryl's car, and I could see her struggling to break free as he lashed out at her. His face was ugly with rage, and he was yelling at her, his hands flying as he hit her. The sight was enough to freeze me in place.

"What the hell is going on?" I heard Aunt Rose's voice, sharp and furious, cutting through the quiet. She charged toward the scene, her face red with anger. "Norman!" she screamed. "What are you doing? You coward!" She moved past him and shoved him hard, knocking him back, but he just sneered at her, ignoring the words that came out of her mouth.

My mom's sisters were livid. They rushed to her side, pulling her away from Norman's grip.

We all piled into the cars and drove home, but the tension in the air was palpable. No one spoke on the way back, except for Norman. He was muttering insults under his breath, but it was clear he was still seething. When we reached the house, Rose finally could not hold it in any longer. She was livid, her face flushed with fury.

"Norman, you're a coward!" she shouted. "You're a bastard for beating up your wife in front of everyone! And to make it worse, you put the baby in danger!" Her voice cracked with emotion, but she didn't back down.

Norman's face twisted, but he didn't respond. Instead, Rose grabbed him by the shirt and shook him. She was livid, tears of frustration streaming down her face. "You think you're tough? Hitting her?!" she yelled. "Let's see how tough you are now!"

Beryl had to step in at that point, pulling Rose away from Norman. "Rose, stop!" Beryl said, her voice firm. "We can't do this here, not like this. You know what will happen if we keep this up. It'll all fall on our sister."

We all went quiet, the weight of Beryl's words sinking in. My mom, Ervin, and I gathered our things quickly. Norman was still drunk, still angry, and we knew we had to leave. We didn't stay another minute. We left that night—the tension between Norman and my mom was so thick it felt suffocating.

The drive home was a nightmare. Norman, barely able to stay upright, so my mom had to drive while he sat in the passenger seat next to her. He would shout at my mom every time she hit the brakes or turned the wheel too sharply. "You're driving too fast," he barked. "You're braking too hard! You're driving too slowly! Why are you letting these damn cars pass us?" His voice, hoarse and angry, was a constant barrage of criticism. He smacked my mom on the back of the head every time she did something he didn't like, his hands slapping the back of her neck with every sharp turn or moment of silence. He hated it when she did not respond, and he hated it when she did respond. His favorite thing to say to her was "Jy vererg my huh? Vererg jy my?" *(You are irritating me huh? Do you dare to irritate me?)* followed by a slap, smack, or punch.

Eventually he decided that he wanted to go and sleep in the back of the bakkie, even if it meant that he would relinquish control of my mom while he was asleep. But somehow, he just could not do it. And so, he told her to stop so he could rejoin her in the front but she would not so he started throwing things out of the window—a water bottle, a pillow, a bag, anything that would catch his attention he sent flying. The night stretched on forever as he raged and swore, throwing threats at my mom, making her feel small and helpless, as though it was somehow her fault for everything that had gone wrong.

The whole trip home was a blur of insults, smacks to the back of the head, and the desperate, silent cries of a family trying to escape the torment.

There was a time when we were going somewhere local, like the beach or to visit family. There were so many incidents and occurrences that I really can't remember the exact details of each and every one. Anyway, true to Norman's nature, he was drunk, and he was spitting vulgarities and obscenities at my mother as per usual. It was a very hot day and Durban is very humid. There wasn't even the slightest breeze, and the air was standing still. But I think on this particular day God thought, "Not today my guy, enough is enough!" The radiator of his car began overheating right then and plumes of steam billowed up from the engine. Norman had to pull the car over to the side of the road to check the engine, all the while swearing at Mom because this too was her fault. He opened the bonnet of the car and removed the radiator cap, and a flood of scalding hot water gushed out and seared his stomach and forearms. He leapt back screaming in agony and instant regret for not letting her remove the cap. His skin was badly burnt, blistering, and peeling.

Finally, Karma had decided to pay him a visit! Norman always wore a shirt with shorts and sandals, so the scalding water flowed down his legs and onto his feet which were also burnt but not as badly as his belly. He was suffering. Deep down in my heart somewhere I felt a bit of a chuckle. Ok, maybe it wasn't so deep. Mom got out to see what had happened and tried to help him. This absolutely insufferable excuse for a human being had the audacity to not even cease his incessant swearing and shouting. It was her fault this happened. Somehow this was her intention all along! He told her to drive him home and fix him. She said he needed to go to the hospital, but he refused. So, she went to the pharmacy to get some supplies and for weeks had to nurse him back to health under a barrage of abuse. It is simply disheartening that despite all the effort invested, not an ounce of appreciation was offered. I kept telling her to leave him, let him see to himself, but she just couldn't or wouldn't do it.

On another occasion, Aunt Rose who lived a few houses down the road from us before moving to

Nigel, was having a house party. Most of her brothers and sisters were there amongst other people and the kids were all playing outside in the yard. It was still early, and the party had barely gotten started when Norman told my mom that it was time to go home. He could not stand to see her enjoying herself. Her sisters asked him to allow her to stay, saying that she would not be home late.

"She is with her family, don't be like that," they said. He backed down because he could never stand up to them. He went home and proceeded to get completely wasted and then came back full of courage. Everyone was on the dance floor, the lights were off, but the disco lights were flashing. He walked in with a torch, which he shone in everyone's faces, calling out her name, "Palmie, Palmie, where are you, damnit? Bitch! Come out now!"

My mother was terrified and so embarrassed. Her sisters banded together and went for him, but my mother begged them not to interfere, knowing that eventually she would have to go home and then the come-uppance would be worse. Better to get it over and done with now instead of later when he got worse and more enraged. So, she left, leaving us kids behind so that we don't have to witness what happened next. It's not like we didn't know anyway.

On a particularly warm sunny day, I was playing in the yard with my two best friends from the neighbourhood. Morgan and Logan were both a few years younger than me, but we were best mates. We mostly played at my house because I was not allowed to go to theirs. If I did go, it was when my parents weren't home, and I had to be sure to get back before they did. So, we were playing in the yard and my parents were arguing in the kitchen. And I peeked in to see what was going on and at that exact moment, Norman's fist struck my mom's face with such jarring force that her teeth and blood went flying through the air. The sound of bone meeting with flesh echoed in the kitchen. It felt like I was watching a slow-motion movie scene. This was such a brutish, cowardly act! I am not sure if it was shock or embarrassment, but I harshly shoved my two surprised besties out of the yard and sent them home without an explanation or a reason. I don't know if they saw what I saw, but they left without too much fuss. By the time I got into the house, Norman was making my mom clean up her own blood and teeth from the floor, and then he took her to the hospital while hurling verbal abuse at her the entire time, because "She made me do it." I cannot imagine the immense amount of pain she was in. I was ten, my brother was four, and we were left alone at home, bewildered and confused.

About a week or two later I was at my aunt's place down the road for the afternoon. That was about the only place I could go freely and for however long I wanted. When I got home, I found the front and back doors wide open and the house empty. The car wasn't in the driveway either. I came back out and found Ethan, the neighbour's son, sitting in their front yard and I asked him if he saw my parents. He nonchalantly answered, "Your dad chased your mom up the road to the soccer grounds with the sjambok, he is in the car, and she was running on foot." He said this so casually that I thought he was joking. Just then another neighbour came walking down the road and said that Norman was chasing my mom round and round the soccer field in his car and some people had gathered to watch.

Chapter 6: Enough is Enough

I was so over it!

I was embarrassed and I was tired.

This was two weeks after she just had her four front teeth smashed out of her mouth, and now this. The humiliation was just never-ending. All I wanted was a moment of respite, free from the never-ending cycle of mortification and weariness. Occasionally after some of the incidents, if they were really bad, he would book himself into rehab and promise that he would never ever do this again, that he loves her so much and he can't live without her.

Oh, he would also promise that he would never interfere with me again either. Because that was one of my mom's major concerns, that he would aways pick on me to start a fight with her. That promise would last for maybe a maximum of six months and then we were back at square one again.

Sometimes he would just quit drinking on his own and then get DT's (delirium tremens), which is a severe side effect of sudden withdrawal from alcohol. One of the many symptoms is hallucinations, which was the worst one that Norman suffered. One of the things he imagined was that he had ants crawling all over his body, so he went to buy a can of Doom chemical insecticide and sprayed his entire body all day long until he thought he no longer saw them. Another time I was playing in the backyard, and the hose pipe was coiled in the corner, but Norman saw a snake and screamed frantically at me to come inside because the snake was about to strike me. And on another occasion, he and my mom had to sleep in my bedroom on the twin beds because he was sweating too much to share a bed. At that time, he thought that they were on two airplanes, and they were flying too close to each other and were going to crash! He was screaming in fear and telling her to fly away from him and that she would kill them both.

But there were times when he just went on endless drinking binges and his narcissistic behaviour was just on another level.

These episodes left us walking on eggshells, never knowing what might trigger his next outburst. The unpredictability of his episodes created an environment of fear and anxiety, where we were always bracing for the next storm. His actions not only strained our relationships but also eroded our sense of self-worth and security.

Every time we or our neighbours would call the police. They would come pick him up and he would spend the weekend in jail. All the police at the local police station were the young men from our neighbourhood, with whom Norman was familiar and with whom Norman often drank. Hence there were never any charges, and he would just be allowed to sober up and was then released. Eventually it would get to a point where they wouldn't even let him sober up, he would just get out of the van at the station and then walk straight back home. It was just too much paperwork to book and charge him with such a petty crime as domestic violence.

So, now he feared nothing. He was even friends with the cops, and it was a joke to them because he could walk home within a matter of 15 minutes and continue where he left off. This was annoying to no end for me and heartbreaking for my mom. She felt helpless and hopeless! Neighbours would actually stand outside in their yard and time him to see how long it would take for him to get back.

Just like I was not given much willpower, I was given even less patience!

My friends and family keep telling me that God continually puts me in certain situations to teach me patience, but I refuse to learn, and so He shall keep putting me in those situations until I have learnt my lesson. It's going to take a while! I have never once claimed to be perfect, and these are but two of my many imperfections.

Norman had this habit of hiding his money and his bottles of alcohol all over the house. And since I was the one who cleaned the house, I would normally find them. I always had, and still have, the need to constantly move furniture and rearrange the rooms in the house and that is how his secrets were revealed. He would hide stuff behind furniture and on top of wardrobes and cupboards or inside linen closets. He hid things inside the ceiling boards or made holes in the back of furniture and stuck stuff in there.

Initially, when I found this alcohol, I gave it to my mom, and she would just throw it out. When Norman realized that it was gone, he would have a fit and accuse us of taking it and of course, for spite he would go and buy double the amount that was thrown out. So, my impatience with situation led me to crush laxatives into fine powder and add it to his liquor instead of throwing it out. Mostly he would not notice and drink it and then get horribly sick with explosive diarrhoea for days, which is exactly what I had intended. But then I became bolder and started to put more and more and then he realized that something was up. He started to inspect his bottles and could see the sediment at the bottom, specifically in the white alcohol. His poison of choice was Mainstay Cane Spirit and Texan Plain cigarettes. But he would drink anything as long as it was alcohol!

Once he figured out that his drink was tampered with, then the fight was on. He would swear and shout and keep my mom awake all night, just badgering her about trying to kill him. On and on he would go. He would fall asleep for a few minutes and then wake up and violently shake her awake, so that he could continue to verbally and mentally torture her until the sun rose, knowing that she was going to work in a few hours. He worked at his brother's company, so he went to work or didn't go to work as it suited him. The lack of sleep was of no consequence to him. But it was a matter of life or death to my mom since her job required her to drive from one site to another all day to check on the staff at the various locations. She had to be alert on the road. Maybe that was his whole point.

Then we learned about a tablet called Anti-booze from his mom. Or so I thought when I was at the age of sixteen. It is in fact called Antabuse or Disulfiram. It is obtainable from a doctor, and it works by blocking the processing of alcohol in the body. This causes you to have a bad reaction when you drink alcohol. Of course, Norman was never going to take this willingly. So, once again, we had to crush it into a fine powder and add it to his food and his alcohol. Boy, did he get sick! But then he became suspicious of absolutely everything. He would watch us dishing his dinner for him to ensure that we didn't put something in the food. He stopped hiding alcohol in the house and hid it outside in the yard or in his car. Every time he wanted a drink he would have to sneak out of the house at all hours of the night and even in the cold to do so. So, the mission was not accomplished, but we did make life a tad more difficult for him.

I mentioned that he also hid his money. Well, I found that too. I would always give it all to my mother and I was always well rewarded for it. He received weekly pay, and the first thing he would do was stop at the bottle store to get his stash for the weekend. When he got home, he would hide the rest of his money in one of his many hiding places and then binge-drink himself into oblivion. This would then leave him with a huge gap in his memory and he would have no idea what he did with his money or where he left it or how he spent it. That is when I would go seek, and I would find! As my reward, my mom would buy me a handbag with matching pumps and sandals, so I had them in abundance in every style and colour that they were available. I was around fourteen and this was great. But at this stage, I was still very much the tomboy. All that prettiness and frilliness was quite lost on me.

I had learned what it felt like to earn my own money, although it was in a rather unconventional way. I started my first business, and I baked cakes and sold them locally, delivering to willing customers in the neighbourhood. Later, I expanded my product list by adding juice concentrates. I did this for three years and then my mom said that it was taking too much time from my studies, so I got a part-time job at a clothing store and worked on Saturdays and school holidays only. I started working at the tender age of thirteen and four decades later I am still going strong.

Chapter 7: Retaliation

As I got older, I also became a lot stronger and bolder in confronting Norman when he began with his shenanigans. I stood up to him more when my mom was not around, because she would never allow it in her presence. Remember, the man is the head of the household. Who am I to backchat and let my opinion be heard loudly and harshly?

So, I did it when she was not home.

Slowly but surely, he began to back down from me and back away from my mom when I was around. Also, at some point, his mom came to live with us. It was for a short period of time because he was just out of control for a while. During this time an incident occurred that shook me to my core because, in everything that had happened prior to this, I never felt as though my life was in danger. My mom maybe, but not me.

I came home from school one day and took off my school shoes in my bedroom, loosened the side zipper of my school uniform, which was a white shirt under a maroon tunic, got my books, and started to do my homework at the dining room table. Normally I would cook dinner for the family, but because my gran was staying with us, she was preparing dinner in the kitchen at that moment.

Norman was drunk, lying on his bed in his underpants. This was his favourite thing to do. He came staggering down the stairs, saw me sitting there mumbled something to himself or it could have been to me, but I chose to ignore him. I think he was angry that I was doing homework and listening to music at the same time. He walked over, put his big hands around my neck, and squeezed. At first, I thought, "This is a new one for the books, this half-naked man standing over me and choking me." And then I realized that this was serious because the look on his face was as if he was looking at an abomination. In fact, he looked like an abomination himself, his face was so twisted and contorted with the strain of applying force to my neck. I tried to push his arms away, but I could not move him at all. I could not make a sound. I started pounding on his chest and at that moment my gran came walking out of the kitchen.

She gasped in horror, not knowing what was going on. All she saw was a child beating her parent. She did not see a parent choking his child! She came over, grabbed my hands, and shouted, "What do you think you doing? You have no respect!"

At this point my eyeballs felt like they were about to pop out of my face, I could not breathe, and I thought, "I am going to die by the hands of these two bastards. Oh, my poor mother!"

I was shaking as his vice-like grip tightened around my throat, cutting off all circulation. The sadism in his eyes sent shivers down my spine. At that terrifying moment survival mode kicked in and as luck would have it, his finger slipped into my mouth as he was squeezing the life out of me, and my jaws just clamped down. With all the defiance I could muster, I sank my teeth into the flesh of his finger, biting down so hard that the blood was running down my chin and neck and into my mouth. Each drop of blood that trickled down was a testament to my tenacity and refusal to back down in the face of adversity. I am not sure if he felt the pain or if it was the sight of the blood that snapped him out of his stupor, but suddenly he stopped, and I yanked my hands away from my gran and I ran out the front door with an unruly urgency while spitting his vile tasting blood out of my mouth. In that very moment, fear became a distant memory as courage took hold of me. Adrenaline surged through my body and my heart pounded against my chest.

I went and sat in the front yard trying to catch my breath and trying to figure out what the hell just happened. I was completely dazed and confused, overwhelmed by the chaos swirling around me, when suddenly, out of nowhere, my knight in shining armour showed up in front of me. At times like this I almost believed that he was born for this purpose. My guardian angel, to protect me, to shield me. For why else would he suddenly appear whenever I needed him the most? God had a plan! Ethan asked, "What happened?" and I shrugged with tears in my eyes, "You know!"

He took me to his house and let me use the bathroom to clean up. I looked in the mirror and what looked back at me was not me. My hair was dishevelled and bushy, my eyes were bloodshot and teary, and there was blood still on my chin and neck and on the collar of my shirt. I looked like something out of a zombie movie. I cleaned up and went downstairs where Ethan was sitting and watching TV. He had a glass of water for me, but he never said a word about the incident. He wasn't one to speak much, especially about what happened in my house. I think he just didn't want to embarrass me. He just told me to stay until my mom got home, then I could leave. And so it was with every occasion that he provided refuge.

There were too many times that Ethan came to my rescue like this. It was as if he possessed an inherent ability to sense when I needed him most, swooping in without hesitation or second thought. With each act of heroism, he solidified his indispensable role in my life, leaving me with an unshakeable gratitude for his unwavering presence. Ethan's constant reassurance reminded me that I was never alone, giving me the courage to face my challenges head-on.

He was two years older than me and both his parents worked, as well as his older sister. During the day he was home alone and the only one there to see what I was going through. Once he left me there alone with a bunch of weapons to protect myself because he had to go somewhere. And another time he was so mad that he offered to go there and beat Norman up because he was tired of seeing me in this situation. On another occasion, Norman threw me out of the house early in the morning just after my mother left for work, but before I was done getting ready for school. I was half-dressed and could not go to school like that. Again, Ethan found me sitting in the front yard when he was on his way to school. He gave me the keys to his house and left me there for the day.

This choking incident made me realise that enough was enough. I was just not prepared to take Norman's crap anymore. So, I back-chatted, ignored, and refused to do what he told me to do. I even stood up to him when my mom was around. He had this habit when he was home on a drinking spree during the week, where he would lay on the bed upstairs and I would be downstairs either doing homework or cooking. He would constantly call me upstairs for silly things. We had the old dial phones, one upstairs on his bedside table and one downstairs in the lounge. If you picked up the receiver on one phone and tapped on buttons underneath it would make a like a "ting-ting" ringing sound on the other phone in the same house. Norman did this constantly to get my attention when he was too drunk to come down the stairs to torture me physically. That sound was annoying, and he would not stop until I went up to see what he wanted.

Sometimes he would be so drunk that he could not even articulate what he was trying to say and other times he would want me to bring him water or light his cigarette or ask who is in the house or where my mother is. He would do this literally every five minutes from the minute I get home from school. One day I was so irate that I blurted out, "What the fuck do you want?" This was after the tenth time of being called. I think we both went into shock then, because we both just stared at each other, him from the bed and me from the doorway to his room. I recovered first and quickly said, "I'm cooking and the food is burning." I turned on my heel and bolted out of there!

That is when he realized that he could not push me around as easily as he did before.

On one of his tirades, he came rushing down the stairs in all his drunken glory because he was calling and calling, and my mom just kept ignoring him after a rough day at work. He decided to come down a teach her a lesson, but the lesson decided to teach him. There was a landing on the top of the staircase as you came off the passage which turned to the left and down the stairs. Then there was a landing at the bottom of the staircase, which turned left to three more steps before reaching the bottom.

He tripped on the top landing, fell straight down headfirst, and slammed his head into the wall at the bottom landing. His right wrist twisted and cracked under weight of his body as he hit the ground. He lay there unconscious. My mom started panicking and I just stood there fascinated. "Is this what karma is" I thought, feeling very satisfied. My mom was so panicked that she called the neighbours, who called the paramedics, and they took him to the hospital. But they asked me to go along with them since he was unconscious, and they needed answers to some questions they had. I was not happy, why did I have to go and help him. It would not have bothered me one bit if he died that day! Alas, he did not.

We were leaving home for the millionth time, and we were packing the car. Because of the steep incline of the street we live in, the houses were built in such a way that each house was situated one step above each other. However, some had a yard above the house before the next house began and ours was such a yard. This is where the driveway was, and where the vehicles parked.

Now we were packing the car, which was a company car my mother had at the time. I was passing the suitcases from the bottom of the yard to the top of the driveway, which was elevated. There was a wall separating the two sections and you could either walk all the way around to the front yard and enter up the stairs or climb the ladder which Norman had placed just outside the front door for ease of access. He was screaming and shouting and demanding that we leave his suitcases that he had bought with his money.

"I bought it, it was my money that bought it. You don't earn enough so you couldn't have bought it with your petty cash and the small change that you earn. Don't you dare leave with anything that that belongs to me woman!" He belittled and berated her. My mom began to cry and the hurt and anger overwhelmed her all at once. Something snapped in the usually calm and passive woman who would just sit and take all the abuse. Suddenly she grabbed the suitcase and emptied the clothes out into the car and threw the case down at him. He was standing in the bottom yard, and she was in the driveway in the top yard. He caught the suitcase and lifted it overhead to throw it back at her. I pushed him with such force that he fell and at the same time my brother, who was normally very passive and stayed hidden during these altercations, charged at him with a panga (also known as a machete, which is a heavy cane knife with a long, broad blade, used as an implement or a weapon). Had I not pushed him, Ervin would have sliced him with that panga right there and then. It must be true that the devil looks after his own! We had all reached our breaking point. Even Ervin, known for his calm disposition, couldn't contain his frustration any longer. It was as if the dam had finally burst, and the flood of pent-up emotions could no longer be contained.

His reaction was unexpected yet unsurprising, a clear indication that we could no longer continue down this path without dire consequences. The weight of our collective stress was suffocating. This dramatic outburst from Ervin served as a wake-up call, an urgent reminder that something desperately needed to change.

Chapter 8: Isolation and Friendship

Because of all this drama and trauma that I was constantly exposed to, I wet the bed until I was seventeen years old. This was a huge embarrassment and I hated sleeping out except for with my family, like at my gran's place on the farm and my aunt's place in Sezela. They were very understanding and they never made a fuss about it.

My mom tried every concoction and home remedy that anyone and everyone ever told her about, including a few drops of Haarlemensis on a teaspoonful of sugar. It was the vilest thing I have ever consumed in my life and probably contributed to my substantial body size.

Sometimes my cousins would tease me about the bedwetting, but they would get into trouble if they got caught. And maybe this is partly why I was never interested in boys romantically.

Norman brought a lot of different men home from the neighbourhood whom he drank with. But by this stage we (Mom, Ervin and I) never brought anyone home, because we were too embarrassed. He would always swear and shout at them in the most vulgar way you can think of, and chase people out of our house like they were animals. It was only his brothers and his drinking buddies that were welcome.

People just did not like coming to our house anyway. It was just too uncomfortable for most of them and there was almost always a backlash after visitors left, so they just stopped coming. At some point, when my cousins still visited, Norman noticed that one of them was developing breasts and I was still flat-chested at the age of fifteen. I am not sure if he saw this as his chance to fondle a young girl and use me as an excuse, but on two occasions he called us over and cupped our breasts. Well, her breasts and my flat chest, and he then berated me for being like a boy and praised her for being like a pretty budding flower, while he had a hand on each of us. After the second time, she never came back again. He never did it to me when I was alone.

My buddy Brody and I have been friends since, I would like to say, birth. I am one or two years older than him, so that is not possible. But we have known each other since we were toddlers. We share a profound connection that transcends the conventional bounds of relationships and even though he left South Africa and travelled the world, we still kept in touch. When he returned our friendship magically picked up exactly where we had left off.

We not only understand each other's struggles but held space for them in ways that provide solace and healing. Our connection is nothing short of extraordinary. It is an unabashed meeting of two souls immersed in a shared intellectual and emotional depth. He was one of those friends who was constantly chased away from our house, but always came back.

Once Norman was so drunk. He heard voices downstairs, mine and Brody's, so he came down in his underwear and chased him out, not politely, screaming and swearing. I was embarrassed and wanted the earth to open up and swallow me whole. At that point I thought I had lost another friend. Because everyone else he had done that to had left, never to return. But Brody calmly walked out to the front yard and when Norman went back upstairs, he came back inside. About twenty minutes later Norman came back down and chased him again, and Brody left and returned. Soon after Norman came back but this time, he walked him out the front gate, still in just his underwear, and watched Brody walk to the corner of the street, then came back inside. Brody stood on the street corner until he saw Norman walk past the bedroom window upstairs and then came back into the house again to hang out with me. At this point, Norman just gave up because he knew he was fighting a losing battle, and this was too much effort in his drunken state.

It is then that I decided that I would do anything for my friend, because he did not give up on me, and he did not abandon me. Neither did he judge me. He was my hero, and he is forever etched in my heart.

> *"A real friend is one who walks in when the rest of the world walks out." — Walter Winchell.*

Chapter 9: Invasion

I was eighteen! There was a steady stream of Norman's friends slithering in and out of the house. I couldn't stand the sight of these sorry specimens stumbling around, reeking of cheap liquor, thinking they were kings of the world and God's gift to all females.

One in particular took a liking to me and continually made sexual innuendos towards me, usually under his breath or behind Norman's back. It is truly astounding how some people can manage to be so repulsive without even realising it or putting any effort into it. He would usually come there during the time I was cooking and find ways to be in the kitchen alone with me. He was married and I would threaten to tell his wife about what he was doing. He would say, "She will never believe you and you know this."

It was true, she loved him so much and she believed anything and everything he told her. She believed that every female wanted her man and that he was the innocent one. More than that, there were so many young men that lived in our street and neighbourhood that believed that I was easy, perhaps because I was a tomboy. They turned me into their target.

Rumours spread and they all competed to see who could sleep with me first. They thought I would be grateful to have someone show interest in me, because I was fat, perhaps. But my self-esteem was not that low. I suffered a lot of verbal and physical sexual abuse from many of them for a very long time and still to this day I often ask myself what did I do to make them think they could do that to me? Did I look desperate or was I enticing them somehow? Maybe they just felt that I needed to be tamed!

I didn't know who to turn to. Norman was useless and what was I supposed to say to my mom on top of everything else she was already dealing with? My best friend Morgan believed me because she had seen him doing and saying these things to me. She offered to hide in a cupboard in order to catch him red-handed, but I was too afraid to get her involved in an elaborate scheme which might fail, and then she would be in trouble too.

That year I finished matric, and Ervin was still in school. He left home in the morning while I was still sleeping and did not lock the door. It just so happened to be one of the days that Norman went to work. I awoke with this heavy weight on top of me. Panicked, I tried to scream but a hand covered my mouth with an intensity that demanded silence. Fear gripped me, its icy fingers wrapping tightly around my chest, making it hard to breathe. My heart pounded so hard that it was deafening, each beat echoing in my ears like a relentless drum. It felt as though my entire body was vibrating with the intensity of my terror, and I could hear nothing but the frantic thudding of my own pulse. Every muscle in my body tensed, ready to run or fight, but I was frozen in place, paralyzed by the overwhelming sense of dread. It was as if the world had shrunk to the size of my own panic, leaving me alone with my racing thoughts and pounding heart.

I realized it was Norman's friend. I was shaking my head vigorously, trying to tell him no, and he was looking in my wide eyes that were now filling with tears. With his other hand he was pulling the blanket out from between us and lifting my nightie. He was relishing in the power he had over me at that moment, his eyes gleaming with a twisted satisfaction. It was as if he drew strength from my vulnerability, savouring every second of my discomfort. His posture exuded confidence and dominance, a stark contrast to my own shrinking presence. The smirk on his face was a clear indication of his enjoyment, a silent proclamation of his control. My fear was fuelling him on. How could someone be so despicable?

He raped me!

When he was done, he said, "Oh I didn't know you were a virgin," with a grotesque grin on his face as the tears rolled down mine.

"You better not tell anyone, because I will completely deny it. Besides, you wanted me to come in, that's why you left the door open for me."

Then he left.

I was dumbfounded, horrified, and terrified!

I was a tomboy; I was flat-chested until age sixteen and then one day I woke up and had huge double-D breasts. I didn't start with training bras like most girls do. I went from nothing to a whole lot in a flash! When they appeared, I started walking hunched over to try and hide them. I did not flaunt them, I hated them! Also, my mom did not explain to me about periods. When it happened and I told her she asked me if my friends had not told me about it. Then she sent me to my aunt to ask for pads. So, I knew even less about sex.

I turned to Morgan, because my greatest fear now was that I was pregnant. But we could not tell anyone about this, so she turned to her two older sisters and innocently asked them questions about what to do in the case of unwanted pregnancy, feigning curiosity. While they were older, they were certainly not wiser. They told her old wives' tales of drinking warm milk with salt and bathing in very hot water with vinegar. Drinking a combination of Lennon's medicines and so on, all of which I tried, none of which worked, I think. Thankfully, I was not pregnant.

Life just continued as if nothing had ever happened. For him at least! For me, life was very different. I was paranoid, I was terrified, and I tried to avoid everyone. This self-imposed isolation only deepened my sense of despair. I felt as though everyone could see that I had had sex. And I felt silently but savagely judged, as if every glance and whisper was a harsh critique of my very being. It was as though people could see right through me, exposing all my deeds and actions. The weight of their unspoken judgements pressed down on me, making it hard to breathe or think clearly.

Norman continued with his drinking spree and my mother continued to live in fear. At this point, I was working part-time and gained a very little bit of freedom. Fifty percent of my salary went to the household, not because they needed it but because that was what we were supposed to do back then.

Later that year Norman stopped drinking and then the DTs kicked in.

On the 1st of December 1987 at 1am we were all in our beds asleep when he awoke and went downstairs to retrieve a knife, came back upstairs, knelt over my mother in her bed, and slit her throat. My mom thought she was dreaming and didn't realise that it was real until it was almost too late. At this stage, she desperately attempted to muster all the strength in her body to call out my name, but only a feeble and pitiful whisper escaped her lips. It was an anguished cry for help. I have always been a light sleeper, and I heard her whisper in my sleep and instinct told me that something was very wrong! I sprang up out of bed and ran down the passage to her room and stood in the doorway in horror as my brain tried to fathom what I was actually seeing. For a second, I thought I was still sleeping and having a nightmare!

Norman was kneeling on the bed with one knee on my mother's chest and one hand holding her two wrists, while she was trying to push the blade of the knife up with her bare hands. He was slicing away at her neck with a huge knife. He did not even seem to notice my arrival at the door of the bedroom. He seemed hell-bent to complete the task at hand.

I did not realize it, but it was at this point that I think I began screaming at the top of my voice as I leaped up on the bed and moved behind him. To me it seemed as if everything was moving in slow motion. I could hear every painful beat of my heart as the panic and fear set in. I put both my arms around his waist and lifted him off my mother with an unwavering determination and strength from the Gods, and shouted, "Run, run, run".

There was no hesitation in my actions, as I was fuelled by a surge of adrenaline and an unyielding sense of protection. I could not see what my mother did, or was doing, because I was turning him away from her at this point. He was trying to loosen my hands, while I had a death grip on him.

In that moment, I became the embodiment of strength and courage, willingly challenging him. He was not the smallest of men, so this was not easy. When I realised that my mom had left the room, I lost power in my grip, and he turned and stuck the tip of the knife in my tummy, just by the belly button. Ervin came running in. There was an umbrella with a duck-head handle leaning against the wall next to the door. He grabbed it and hit the knife out of Norman's hand just as it cut into my skin. I was shouting at him, "Run, run, Ervin. Get out of the house and go find mummy!" The knife had fallen to the floor, and I managed to get in front of Norman because he wanted to chase after my mother. I got to the top of the staircase, and I sat down and spread my arms across the stairway so that he could not pass. He was furious at me and started kicking my lower back with his thick-soled shoes. All the while I was clenching my teeth in agony, but I refused to budge.

"You fat bitch, who do you think you are to stop me? Get out of my way, you stupid cow. Move before I kill you, stupid bitch," he roared, enraged. I didn't know the condition my mom was in or where she was. I just sat there steadfastly, determined to buy her as much time as I possibly could.

Then my neighbour, Ethan's mom, came in and grabbed me by the hand and ran out with me, telling me my mom would be ok.

Chapter 10: Beginning of the End

When I got outside, I was shocked to see the entire neighbourhood standing outside in their pyjamas and sleepwear, watching what was going on. There were at least thirty people just standing around trying to see what was going on. I mean it was around 2 am for Pete's sake.

I asked one of my friends why they were there, and he said, "You were screaming so loud that you woke everyone up."

He lived quite a distance away from my house. We got into Ethan's house and then I saw my mom for the first time. She was in the bathroom with blood-soaked towels around her neck and blood was surging out when she lifted the towels. The gruesome sight nearly broke me, but I had to stay strong for my mom. I was enraged that we had gotten to this!

Finally, he had actually tried to kill her. I always knew it would happen. Ethan's sister was calling the police and the paramedics and trying to find some clothes for us to wear since we just got out of our house in nighties and pjs. I asked where Norman was and what he was doing, and they said that he had locked himself inside the house.

At this time the paramedics had arrived and administered some first aid to my mom, then put her in the ambulance and taken her to the hospital. I had climbed into the ambulance with her, since she had now gone into shock and could not communicate effectively anymore.

Aunt Rose came to fetch Ervin and they followed us to the hospital with the neighbours. It took a very long time for my mom to get treatment and we sat in the waiting room. While we were there the police came to look for me to ask what had happened. After explaining the events of the night, he told me that after we had gotten out of the house, Norman cut both his arms on the outer part just below the elbow and proceeded to bleed throughout the entire house. He bled on the walls, floors, and carpets of all the rooms, except for my bedroom and the kitchen.

I was flummoxed! I am not sure what exactly was the aim of that, but I did mention that he was very intelligent and rather manipulative! At about 9am, while my mom was still in treatment, the other police brought him down the passage after he had received stitches on his superficial wounds.

When he saw me, he pretended to be dazed and confused. "May, what's wrong, what's going on? Why are we here?" he asked in a childlike voice and a very condescending manner.

That is when I decided that forgiveness does not live here!

The intensity of my anger was so overwhelming that it felt as though the sheer pressure building within my skull would cause it to burst open. My temples throbbed with a relentless, pounding ache, and every heartbeat seemed to amplify the fury coursing through my veins. It was as if a storm had been unleashed inside me, with waves of rage crashing against the fragile walls of my composure.

My vision blurred, tinged with red, as the anger clouded my thoughts and made it difficult to focus on anything else. Each breath I took was shallow and rapid, feeding the fire that burned within me. My fists clenched involuntarily, nails digging into my palms as I struggled to contain the explosive energy threatening to erupt.

The sensation was almost physical, a tangible force that demanded release. It felt like my head was a pressure cooker, the steam building up to a point where it could no longer be contained. The urge to scream, to lash out, to do something—anything—to alleviate the unbearable tension was nearly irresistible.

Waves of infuriation surged through every inch of my being, threatening to consume my rationality and self-control entirely.

If the cops were not there at that time I would have violently attacked and mauled him right there and then.

His insolence and disregard for basic decency had pushed me to the absolute brink.

Oh, how I longed to let loose my pent-up fury upon his wretched being! Not only for what had happened that night, but for the twenty years of torture that we had endured! No ounce of mercy would have spared this vile creature if circumstances allowed it.

As I sit here writing this now, thirty-six years later, I can still feel the anger of that moment well up inside of me as tears fill my eyes.

I turned around and walked away without saying a word to him. He was taken away to jail while my mom was still being treated. She received nineteen stitches on the throat, but she also had to be stitched internally, because she was cut right down to the trachea and her vocal cords sustained some damage. She also received stitches on her fingers on both hands. When we left the hospital, we spent a few days at Aunt Rose's place, because Mom required bed rest and I was working at my part-time job. Ervin was still at school.

When mom had recovered enough, we went back home, but boy were we in for a surprise! The putrid stench of blood that lingered in every corner of the house, the pungent odour that simply refused to dissipate, was the lamentable consequence of Norman's reprehensible actions. All the blood-soaked mattresses, carpets, curtains were removed but the foul smell was horrendous. For years afterwards, I could smell it everywhere, like it was on my skin and in my hair. It clung to me like an unwelcome ghost, haunting every waking moment with its acrid presence. We had to repaint the house and deep clean everything, but I could still smell it.

Norman was arrested and charged with attempted murder by the state.

He found himself a lawyer as cunning as himself and he pleaded temporary insanity. He was sent to a psychiatric hospital for a month, to assess his mental capacity. He won his case!

I have lived with this man my entire life and have witnessed and have been manipulated by him countless times and thus know when he is acting and lying. Trust me, he was lying! I have seen his deceitful ways, his talent for distorting reality to serve his own sinister agenda. He was of sound mind enough to cut himself superficially in order to mess the house with his blood to make it look like he was insane just after he attempted murder. Now he claimed temporary insanity; and to prove his case, for an entire month he acted insane while in the psychiatric hospital.

As soon as he came out of that hospital, he was suddenly perfectly sane, because he had achieved his goal. He still had the audacity to come to me after the court case to thank me for saving him. I did no such thing, but that was his way of rubbing it in my mom's face that she had lost.

While he was in the hospital, my mom divorced him and was awarded the house and custody of Ervin who was still a minor at the time.

For a long time, my mother and Ervin lived in fear and went about their daily lives hoping that they didn't run into him. Me, I survived on anger!

I walked around hoping to see him. My anger towards him became the source of my torment and my liberation. For the longest time I demanded retribution for all that he had put us through and all that he had taken from us. I played different scenarios over and over in my head of what I would do if I saw him, how I would react, and what I would say. My thoughts became a playground for the darkest corners of my imagination, fuelling my desire for vengeance. As each day passed, my heart grew heavier with anger and resentment, seeking an opportunity to confront him face-to-face. I dreamt of a grand confrontation where justice would finally be served. I was twenty now, and I was not afraid of him.

Chapter 11: Adjustment

A year had passed since the rape and the attempted murder had taken place.

Norman had moved away and after bothering us for a short while, he eventually gave up and we just went on with our lives as best we could.

Mom was working. Ervin was schooling. I was working as a doctor's assistant not far from home. I used to walk to and from work every day. I alternated shifts with my colleague, so one week I worked from 8am to 2pm and the following week from 1pm to 7pm. I did not have a boyfriend since the incident and so I always walked alone.

One day I was on my way home after my shift at 2pm, when an Indian guy in a Mercedes Benz stopped across the street from me to ask for directions. I really thought he was lost because he was an Indian in a Coloured township which was not very common in those days.

Sometimes it was quite dangerous for Indians to come into Coloured territory, especially if the gangsters saw him. So, I tried to help as quickly as possible. I stood there and started explaining to him which route he should take, without looking at him because I was looking in the direction I was pointing. When I did look back at him to see if he understood me, I saw that this guy was masturbating right there in front of me while I was talking. I was shocked and flustered, my words caught in my throat as if gripped by an invisible force.

Such was the overwhelming impact of this encounter that it drained me entirely, rendering mere words inadequate to encapsulate the storm brewing within me. The unexpected turn of events caught me off guard, my mind scrambling to comprehend what had just transpired. As my mouth hung open in mute surprise, I could feel the blood draining from my face. Time seemed to stand still as I struggled to regain my composure, desperately attempting to process the magnitude of the situation. The guy who was leaning his head out of the window, and holding a white handkerchief in one hand, said, "Please don't stop talking, keep talking, please say something, please, please." All while heavy breathing.

I turned to walk away in utter disgust. "Don't go, please don't go," he said breathlessly.

I started running. I was shaking.

This was another thing that I just kept to myself. For how do I even begin to tell someone this? It was yet another burden that only I could bear, another truth so agonizingly intimate that it seemed impossible to articulate. And who would believe me? Why were all these kinds of things happening to me? Was I doing something to attract this kind of behaviour? These questions consumed my thoughts as I contemplated the inexplicable series of events that seemed to befall me. Yet, in a bold and confident tone, I refused to succumb to self-blame or victimhood.

After a few years, at the age of twenty-one, whilst still being somewhat of a tomboy, I got my first real boyfriend.

What attracted me to him most was the fact that he was a biker, and I just loved the thrill of riding a motorbike. The relationship didn't last too long. As a result of all my past unresolved trauma my relationships were destined to be dysfunctional anyway.

Shortly thereafter, I left Durban and went to find work in Johannesburg. I lived with Aunt Beryl for a short while. It wasn't long before I found a job and was amazed at what seemed to be a huge amount of money at the time. It was a lot compared to what I had earned in Durban.

I continued to support my mother and brother financially and soon moved out from Beryl's place and shared a flat with a co-worker. Shortly thereafter, I met the man who became my first husband. He was the caretaker of the block of flats that we lived in and we developed a friendship and ultimately became romantically involved.

As far as that is concerned, I believe that we all make mistakes. What's done is done.

"So, cry for a little while, keep your regrets short, but remember it for a long time. And soon you won't be disappointed in yourself anymore!" – Anonymous

These are words I live by. Nevertheless, before we got married, I went with him to Durban once and we ran into Norman in the street.

I was over my need for justice and revenge plots at this stage. More out of spite than courtesy, I told Norman that this was my boyfriend. Norman was trying to act all fatherly and interrogate him, and I shut him down.

Who the hell did he think he was? He does not get to play any kind of role in my life at all, period!

It is a declaration that emanates from the depths of my soul, fuelled by years of anger, betrayal, and heartache.

I stand resolute in my decision to sever all ties with him, denying him the privilege of witnessing the milestones and celebrations that define my existence. He is relegated to a mere spectator on the sidelines of my vibrant journey through life; an insignificant character destined for oblivion. The curtain has fallen on our relationship; there will be no encore for him.

Now and then I would receive a call from my mom to say that Norman has done this, or Norman is doing that. Then I would call him and threaten him rather harshly and he would stop his nonsense for a while. That is when I realised that he was now afraid of me. That permanently altered how I spoke to him. It was no longer a daughter speaking to her father. I was speaking to a man for whom I had the utmost contempt and not one ounce of respect.

I would hate him, but it took too much effort.

I was also adamant that he would never meet my kids, he was just not worthy!

Once he tried to sell my mom's house without her knowing. She came home from work and found a *For Sale* board in front of the house. Upon calling the estate agent, she found out that he had put the house up for sale. I called him with a slew of profanities and threats.

We never heard from him again until he died of cancer in the year 2000.

In between all that, I have tried to live my own life as best I can, for I refuse to be overshadowed or controlled by the chaos that surrounded me. It is said that hurt people hurt people, and that the abused often become abusers. With a grateful heart, I can say that neither Ervin nor I are products of our father's wicked and evil behaviour. Instead, we embody our mother's love, perseverance, and resilience.

But I am more than just a survivor. Over the years, I have transformed pain into power, learning skills that have helped me heal and thrive. I've mastered the art of self-awareness—being honest with myself about my feelings, my fears, and my triggers. Journaling and writing this story became a sacred space where I could untangle the knots of my past and find clarity in the present.

I've also leaned into the strength of choice. Every day, I make the conscious decision not to let my past define me. I've chosen forgiveness—not for Norman, but for myself—to free my spirit from the weight of anger and resentment. Forgiveness does not excuse what happened, but it allows me to reclaim my power.

Building boundaries has been another cornerstone of my healing. I've learned to say no—to people, to situations, and to relationships that don't serve my well-being. Protecting my peace became a priority, and with that came the realisation that I deserved happiness, safety, and love.

Mindset has been my greatest ally. I stopped seeing myself as a victim of circumstances and started identifying as a creator of opportunities. I was always a fighter, in any case.

I began to trust in my ability to adapt, to endure, and to grow. Gratitude, even in the smallest of things, became my daily practice. It reminded me that, despite everything, life still held moments of beauty and joy.

With unwavering determination and an unshakeable belief in my potential, I have carved out a path of greatness amidst the tumultuous tides of existence. I choose defiance; to break free from constraints and forge my destiny on my own terms. Through trials and tribulations, I rise above adversity, harnessing every setback as fuel for resilience and perseverance.

The burden of being me weighs heavy, but it also gives my life purpose. I am my mother's keeper. I am my brother's keeper. And now, I am my own keeper.

My mother's coping mechanism for all the trauma she has endured is to forget. She hardly remembers most of the events that took place, and what she does remember is often distorted. While I cannot erase her pain, I have chosen to honour her sacrifice by becoming a beacon of strength and compassion.

I have asked myself a million times, as I am sure most of us have, what is my purpose in life? Why was I born? My answer is this: I was born to rise, to inspire, and to travel beyond the limits of my past. Through growth, healing, and courage, I've become the architect of my own life—a testament to the power of perseverance.

The world calls to me like an open book, with pages waiting to be written in every language, every landscape, every culture. Travel has always been my sanctuary and my classroom, a place where I rediscover myself amidst the unfamiliar. I dream of walking ancient streets, feeling the pulse of cities that hum with life, and standing in awe of nature's grandeur on mountaintops and along endless shores.

My vision for the future is bold and boundless. I see myself as a citizen of the world, embracing its diversity, its challenges, and its beauty. My love of travel fuels my curiosity and reminds me that every journey is a chance to heal, to grow, and to connect. With every plane ticket and every new stamp in my passport, I reclaim the freedom that was once denied to me.

I envision a life where I am not just a survivor but a storyteller, using my experiences to inspire and uplift others. I want to walk into rooms filled with voices from around the globe, sharing my truth and listening to theirs, finding the threads that bind us as human beings. Travel will not only be an adventure but a bridge—to cultures, to understanding, and to healing.

I see myself building a legacy rooted in compassion, resilience, and exploration. I'll write about my travels, weaving the landscapes of the world with the landscapes of my soul. I'll create spaces—both physical and metaphorical—where people can come together to share their stories, to heal, and to dream.

Most of all, I see freedom—freedom to explore the world without fear, to live fully without apology, and to love deeply without restraint. I see a future where my passport becomes a symbol of everything I've overcome and every horizon I've yet to reach.

I carry my mother's spirit, my brother's loyalty, and my own hard-won strength into this future. The weight of my past may travel with me, but it no longer defines me. It becomes a reminder of how far I've come and how much farther I'm destined to go.

The road ahead is uncertain, but I welcome it. Because no matter where I stand, whether beneath the Northern Lights or in the heart of a bustling city square, I know this: I am home in myself. And that is a freedom worth chasing to the ends of the earth.

Epilogue

My story is a powerful testament to resilience, love, and the unyielding spirit that refuses to be broken. My journey has been marked by both pain and triumph, moments of despair and deep joy, shaping me into the person I am today.

Despite the hardships I've faced, I carry forward the love and strength instilled in me by my mother. She taught me the value of perseverance, even in the face of overwhelming odds. Her unwavering belief in me gave me the courage to keep going, striving to live a life of purpose and fulfilment.

Standing up to my father's abuse and fighting for my family's safety took every ounce of courage I had. It meant defying a man who was supposed to protect me, facing a system that often turns a blind eye to abuse, and reclaiming my voice in a world that tried to silence me.

Along the way, I learned to accept myself, embracing my body and my identity in a way I never thought possible. Healing didn't come overnight. It was a process—long, messy, and at times unbearable. But in the end, it was worth every step.

The Reality of Abuse

Too many children grow up in broken and abusive homes, with parents or caregivers battling alcoholism, mental illness, or their own unresolved trauma.

The effects are far-reaching, touching every part of their lives. This includes:

- **Emotional Scars:** Low self-esteem, trust issues, and a constant sense of unworthiness.
- **Behavioural Patterns:** A tendency to repeat cycles of abuse or addiction, and to choose life partners who echo the patterns of their original abusers.
- **Mental Health Challenges:** Anxiety, depression, and PTSD.
- **Physical Effects:** Chronic illnesses stemming from prolonged stress.

Not everyone has the indomitable will to rise above these challenges as I did. But healing is possible. It starts with support—friends, family, therapy, and sometimes just one person who believes in you.

What Helps Us Heal?

- Access to therapy and counselling.
- Building a support network of trusted individuals.
- Recognising and naming the abuse.
- Practicing self-care and forgiveness— especially self-forgiveness.
- Educating others to prevent cycles of abuse. Speaking up and speaking out!

For me, the friends and family who stood by me during my darkest hours were my lifelines. Many of the things I endured happened behind closed doors, in silence and shame. But by speaking up, leaning into the discomfort, and refusing to accept abuse as "normal," I found freedom.

How Can YOU Help?

Every and any person you meet could be living a story like mine. Abuse isn't always visible, but there are signs to watch for:

- Unexplained injuries or frequent absences.
- Withdrawal from social interactions.
- Fearfulness around certain people or places.
- Sudden changes in behaviour or academic performance.

For children this includes:

Physical Signs

- Frequent or unexplained bruises, burns, cuts, or fractures.
- Injuries in patterns (e.g., handprints, belts, or ropes).
- Wearing long sleeves or pants in warm weather to hide injuries.
- Untreated medical or dental issues.

Behavioural Signs

- Sudden changes in behaviour or extreme mood swings.
- Regression to earlier behaviours (e.g., bedwetting, thumb-sucking).
- Fearfulness, especially around specific people or situations.
- Reluctance to go home or fear of leaving school.
- Aggression or hostility toward others, including peers.
- Overly compliant, passive, or withdrawn behaviour.
- Acting out sexually or using explicit language beyond their age.

Emotional Signs

- Low self-esteem or feelings of worthlessness.
- Anxiety, depression, or excessive worry.
- Difficulty forming relationships or trusting others.
- A lack of interest or withdrawal from activities they once enjoyed.
- Expressing feelings of guilt or self-blame.

Educational Signs

- Frequent absences or tardiness without explanation.
- Difficulty concentrating or sudden drop in academic performance.

- Wearing the same clothes repeatedly, often unwashed.

Neglect Indicators

- Poor hygiene or consistently dirty clothing.
- Malnutrition or frequent hunger.
- Unattended medical needs (e.g., untreated injuries or illnesses).
- Being left alone or unsupervised for long periods.

Social Signs

- Limited interactions with peers or a lack of friends.
- Avoidance of physical contact or flinching at sudden movements.
- Reluctance to share personal experiences or secrets.

Environmental Clues

- Living conditions that are unsafe, unsanitary, or overcrowded.
- A parent or caregiver showing little interest in the child's well-being.
- Witnessing parental substance abuse or domestic violence.

Other Warning Signs

- Frequent unexplained accidents or injuries.
- Child seems hyper-vigilant or overly alert, as if anticipating danger.
- Displays knowledge of sexual topics inappropriate for their age.
- Running away from home or frequently attempting to do so.

If you suspect child abuse, it's crucial to report your concerns to the appropriate authorities or child protection services. Even if you're unsure, professionals can investigate and ensure the child's safety.

If you see these signs, don't look away. Speak up, offer support, and connect them with resources that can help.

If You've Suffered Trauma or Abuse

You don't have to face it alone. There are options:

- Reach out to trusted friends or family members.
- Seek professional help through therapy or counselling.
- Join support groups with others who understand your experience.

Remember that healing is a journey—it's okay to take it one step at a time.

And no matter how dark it gets, there is always hope. The things that try to break us only succeed if we let them. Survival is about getting up one more time than you're knocked down. You don't have to do it alone—help is available.

Resources for Help

In South Africa:

Childline: 0800 055 555

POWA (People Opposing Women Abuse): 011 642 4345

SAPS (South African Police Service): 10111

Internationally:

National Domestic Violence Hotline (USA): 1-800-799-7233

Childline UK: 0800 1111

Lifeline Australia: 13 11 14

Together, we can break the chains of pain and create a world where no child has to grow up in fear.

Made in United States
North Haven, CT
09 May 2025

68706258R00062